Eden

THE LITTLE DESIGNER GUIDES

BEAUTIFUL THINGS TO MAKE WITH
BEAUTIFUL FABRIC

nel

ART FOR LIVING

Eden
The Little Designer Guides

First published in Great Britain in 2013 by
Quail Publishing
www.quailpublishing.co.uk

Designs: Nel Whatmore with the help of Margaret Rowan,
Christine Down and Kath Allaway
Photography: Heidi Coppock Beard
Graphic Design: Darren Brant

ISBN 978-0-9567851-5-2

Printed in the United Kingdom

www.nelpatterns.com

CONTENTS

THE FIRST

'LITTLE DESIGNER GUIDE'

Okay, here is a little background on me for those that are interested! If not, then feel free to skip ahead to the projects and the ideas of what you can do with Eden, my latest collection.

I have been a painter for twenty five years and am fortunate that people seem to still love what I do, for which I am very thankful. Nothing makes me happier (at least at work!) than spending my time painting, playing loud music in my studio and making a mess.

I paint in pastel most of the time, although I do use oils too. Colour is my main motivation, plus the need to convey emotions that are often hard to express. I looooove colour! I love how it can lighten the heart and raise a smile.

I was born in Wolverhampton and did Foundation Art and Design at what was then Wolverhampton Poly, where I had the best year of my education, and can remember laughing far more than I had ever done before. I treasure doing many things for the first time that year – and before anyone's imagination runs away with them my list includes life drawing, painting gorillas and chimpanzees at Dudley Zoo, and (most significantly) discovering pastels.

Since then, to give you a potted history, I have done a degree in Communications and Media at Trinity and All Saints College in Leeds, which I actually didn't enjoy that much. However, whilst there, I met my husband Mark who was in the year above. He asked me to marry him as I had a terrible day, and I said yes! I had an elastic band for a ring and got a real one four years later when, having struggled for several years to establish himself as a writer, he finally sold his first book. A quarter of a century later we have two lovely children and we're still making a living out of writing and art. We both work very hard but thankfully still love what we do.

I started designing fabric for Freespirit about five years ago after approaching Westminster Fibres to ask whether they would be interested in me designing a range of textiles for them. Much to my surprise they said yes! So I had to learn how to do it very quickly – it was a real baptism of fire! With every new collection I learn more about textiles, quilting, sewing and putting patterns into repeat. It's been a steep but enjoyable learning curve, and continues to be so. I don't claim to be an expert by any stretch of the imagination, but like a lot of people I like making nice things. I aim for simplicity, but also want to produce something that looks different and eye catching. Hence "The Little Designer Guides", which tell the story of each collection – from what inspired the collection, to what you can make with it, and also simply what goes with what. I hope that you enjoy them and find them useful.
If you want to see all the latest news go to facebook.com/nelpatterns

Nel x

INSPIRATION FOR THE COLLECTION

FROM INSPIRATION  TO PAINTING  TO DESIGN  TO PATTERN

With Eden the answer to the eternal question 'What inspired the collection?' is simple. For the last seven years I have been lucky enough to exhibit at the world famous Chelsea Flower Show. It's very hard work, but a very wonderful experience and an annual source of inspiration to me.

On the shows open days thousands upon thousands of people flood to London to see the gardens and exhibits from all over the world. But on the Sunday before the show opens, I always stay late and spend a few very treasured hours roaming around the show ground and gardens gathering inspiration, taking photos and doing sketches for paintings for the following year. Eden is inspired by one such garden, I saw on that Sunday, two years ago, it was designed by Cleve West and it won Best in Show.

There was something special about it as it radiated a lovely warmth and calmness which drew me to it. I painted an original pastel of it and developed the Eden master pattern from it.

The final stage is to work out the other two colourways which I can only describe as a visual juggling act, when you try to balance scales of patterns, colours and structure to create a nice balance. It's a labour of love!

Cleve West's Garden

Eden my Original Painting inspired by Cleve West's Garden

Eden Master Design in eighteen colours

Ideas and Palette to compliment the main pattern

EDEN FABRIC

THE KEY FOR THE PATTERNS

Fabrics by *FreeSpirit*

PWNW029 Eden - Brown
Fabric 1

PWNW029 Eden - Green
Fabric 2

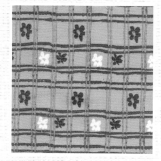

PWNW032 Picnic Check - Pink
Fabric 3

PWNW032 Picnic Check - Green
Fabric 4

PWNW032 Picnic Check -
Strawberry   Fabric 5

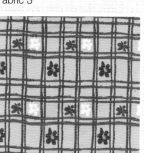

PWNW032 Picnic Check - Peach
Fabric 6

PWNW030 Blossom- Green
Fabric 7

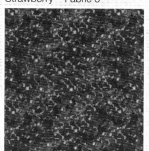

PWNW030 Blossom- Pink
Fabric 8

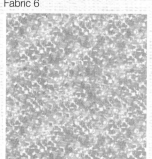

PWNW030 Blossom- Peach
Fabric 9

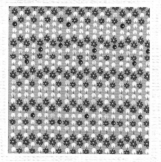

PWNW033 Daisy Chain - Green
Fabric 10

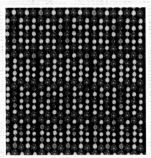

PWNW033 Daisy Chain - Brown
Fabric 11

PWNW033 Daisy Chain - Peach
Fabric 12

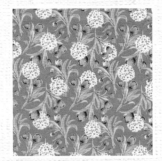

PWNW034 Spring - Slate
Fabric 13

PWNW034 Spring - Pink
Fabric 14

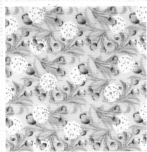

PWNW034 Spring - Green
Fabric 15

PWNW031 Cherry - Dark Brown
Fabric 16

PWNW031 Cherry - Green
Fabric 17

PWNW031 Cherry - Peach
Fabric 18

PWNW031 Cherry - Light Brown
Fabric 19

Free Spirit Designer Solid S58
Fabric 20

Free Spirit Designer Solid S42
Fabric 21

Cream

TWEETERS
TWEET, TWIT, TWOO

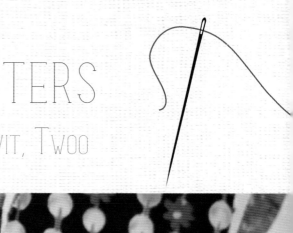

Plain and simply I just wanted to make something that made me smile every time I looked at them. So here are my little Tweet, Twit and Twoo, who are currently sitting on my bookshelf.

Finished Size
20cm x 20cm (8"x8") approx
PLEASE NOTE READ ALL PATTERN INSTRUCTIONS BEFORE STARTING

PLEASE NOTE THESE BIRDS ARE DECORATIVE ONLY AND SHOULD NOT BE USED AS TOYS AS THE WIRE DOES MAKE THESE BIRDS UNSUITABLE FOR YOUNG CHILDREN.

Note Re Material Quantity
Please note: *The quantity of fabric listed below will give you more than enough to make three birds. But as this is the minimum that you can buy this is what I have suggested. It is a great way to use up scraps of fabric, which is what I was trying to do. (You could also make the Birds of A Feather Flock Together Cushion with the leftover fabric although you will also need a few other fat qtrs if you wish to make it look exactly like the cushion depicted, please see pattern.)*

Fabric Requirements

Fat qtr of **Fabric 1**
Fat qtr of **Fabric 8**
Fat qtr of **Fabric 11**
Fat qtr of **Cream**
Fat qtr of **Fabric 21**

You will also need
60 x 50cm (20 x 24") fabric to fabric bonding (Bondaweb Heavy, Heat and Bond or similar) (Suitable for ironing on and bonding two fabrics together firmly)
Contrasting thread for appliqué
Small bag of toy wadding
2.8m (9ft 2") 1mm wire (for each bird) Covered green garden wire . *Please note* *I used 1mm wire, which means you have to spend a little time making your birds stand up as the wire is more delicate. You could use up to 2mm wide wire, which gives greater stability but makes the feet look more chunky. So it's a bit of a trade off, and I will leave it up to you. I wanted more delicate feet.*
Embroidery thread for eye detail optional

"TWOO"

"TWEET"

"TWIT"

Tweet

1

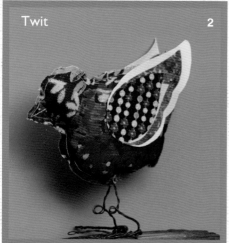

Twit

2

Twoo

3

Paper Pattern Pieces
Photocopy and cut out of paper, 1 Bird Body, 2 Large Bird Wings, 1 Medium Wing and I Small Wing all at 100%

For 'Tweet' cut out the following
Tweet Body – Fabric Freespirit – Chocolate – Fold fabric over and pin Bird Body to fabric. Cut out Bird giving you 2 bodies.
Tweet Head - Fabric 11 - Fold fabric over and pin Bird Head to fabric. Cut out head, giving you 2 heads.
Tweet Wings - Cream - Fold fabric over and pin 2 Large Bird Wings to fabric. Cut out wings, giving you 4 large wings.
Tweet Wings - Fabric Freespirit – Chocolate
Tweet Wings - Fabric 1 Fold fabric over and pin Medium Wing to fabric. Cut out wing, giving you 2 wings.

For 'Twit' cut out the following
Twit Body - Fabric 1- Fold fabric over and pin Bird Body to fabric, cut out Bird Body, this will give you a front and back body.
Twit Wings - Cream -Fold fabric over and pin 2 Large Bird Wings and 1 Small Wing to fabric. Cut out wings, giving you 4 large and 2 small wings.
Twit Wings - Fabric 8 - Fold fabric over and pin Medium Bird Wing to fabric. Cut out wing, giving you 2 wings.
Twit Wings - Fabric 11 - Fold fabric over and pin Small Wing to fabric. Cut out wing, giving you 2 wings.

For 'Twoo' cut out the following
Twoo Body - Cream - Fold fabric over and pin Bird Body to fabric. Cut out body, giving you 2 bodies.
Twoo Heads- Fabric 8 Fold fabric over and pin Bird Head to fabric.
Cut out head, giving you 2 heads.

Twoo Wings - Fabric 1 Fold fabric over andpin Medium Wing to fabric. Cut out wing, giving you 2 wings. Repeat so you end up with 4 wings.
Twoo Wings – Fabric 8 Fold fabric over and pin Medium Wing to fabric. Cut out wing, giving you 2 wings. Repeat so you end up with 4 wings.

Twoo Wings - Fabric Freespirit - Chocolate - Fold fabric over and pin Medium Wing to fabric. Cut out wing, giving you 2 wings. Repeat so you end up with 4 wings.

<u>Sewing & Making Instructions</u>

Step 1 Wings

Before going further check that you have the correct wings cut out for each side of your bird. No bird needs two right wings! The wings should be a mirror of each other when you lay them out.
Place Bondaweb or Heat & Bond or similar product sticky face up or rougher side up on a flat surface, lay all wings and bird heads on top right side up. Pin carefully and cut a Bondaweb or Heat & Bond shape out for all wings and heads.
Then put a sheet of newspaper with an old sheet or a piece of material over the top, on your ironing board, to prevent you getting a sticky ironing board. Turn all wings and heads over so that the sticky side of the Bondaweb is face down on top of the wrong side of your material, iron in place. Please note that for Tweet and Twit you only need to put Bondaweb on two of the cream wings not all four as you will be sticking the other cream one to it. Similarly with Twoo, each of the three wing segments will need to be stuck to its' pair, so you need only stick Bondaweb to 6 wings (three on each side not all 12!). Peel off the protective backing that you have just ironed on. Additionally cut out 10 small wing Bondaweb wings shapes.

Step 2 Assemble Wings

For **Tweet**- firstly place large cream wing Bondaweb side up on ironing board match cream wing with no Bondaweb to it. Iron the 2 cream wings together and repeat for the other 2 cream wings. Then position your Medium Wing then 2 small wings as per **Pic 1**. Iron those all together.
For **Twit**- Repeat as per above for cream wings then add the 2 Medium Wings
For **Twoo**- match each wing up with its' Bondaweb partner and iron together.
You need to join the 3 wings together on each side.

You do this by ironing one of the small Bondaweb wing shapes, in between each layer, like a sandwich. Fan the wings slightly as per **Pic 3** so you can see each wing before ironing together.

All wings should now be joined. Using your last 6 small wing bondaweb pieces iron them to back of each wing towards the rounded end of the wing. Peel off backing, then position them on Bird Body and iron on each side of your three birds.

Step 3 Bird Bodies

For **Tweet** and **Twoo** Iron Bird Heads to each side of your two birds matching the edges up with the head on the body.

All seam allowances are 1cm or 3/8" unless otherwise stated.

For all 3 birds - Put 2 wrong sides of bird's bodies together and pin a 1 cm seam all the way around. I decided to do the seam on the outside rather than turning the bird inside out, as I liked it as a feature of the bird's design, just in case anyone was wondering! So I would suggest using a contrasting thread to machine sew the bodies together, as that makes more of a feature of it. Do a little indentation for the beak see **Pic 2**. Leave a 2" sized gap at the base of the bird to stuff it. They are quite easy to stuff but if you find it difficult to stuff the head just use a pencil or knitting needle to help you. If you want your bird to have an eye, just use embroidery thread and do a large French knot on each side of the head.

Step 4 Join wings to Body
Using your last 6 small wing Bondaweb pieces iron them to back of each wing towards the rounded end of the wing. Peel off backing, then position them on Bird Body and iron on.

Step 5 Only the feet to Go!
See **Step by Step** illustration on **Page 15**
To make all three birds cut six 1.4m (55") lengths of the green garden wire. 1.4m for each foot.
A Fold wire in two around a pencil to create a loop at

the end. Remove pencil. Place loop and wire flat down on a surface. Pretend that there is a clock flat down on the surface and the heel of your bird is the centre of the clock. **B** Point the first loop at 12 o'clock. Twist wire for 6 cm, in the direction of the centre of the clock, towards you (the bird's heel) making sure it is still flat on the surface. To create the second claw, bend the wire around your pencil to create another loop, twist loop to secure. **C** Then virtually bend the wire back on itself again for 6cm (2 3/8") in the direction of 10 o'clock.

Then bend the two wires back again creating a loop around the pencil at the end, before doubling back to the centre (heal), twist the four lengths of wire to create the second claw, leaving the loop at the end.

Thread the two cut ends of the wire down through the loop at the heal. **D** Again, bend wire back on itself and up to 2pm on your imaginary clock.

Wrap wire around your pencil and then back down to your heel. Twist all four wires again. Make sure all three claws are parallel with your flat surface, adjust them if they are not. Then take the two cut ends and thread them from below and up through the pencil loop you have created in the heel.

If you need to in effect thread the two cut wires through the heel again to make the claws stable then that's fine. **E** Then twist the two wires for approx 5cm (2"), go around your pencil with both wires to create the bird's knee. Repeat this for the other foot, then place two feet on a flat surface. Bend them into shape so that they stand up. Bend knees over feet at about 45 degrees. **F** Then twist the two wires of each foot together 4cm (1 ½") above the knees.

I must emphasise that this is very approximate and if you want your bird to have longer legs or straighter ones then no one is going to stop you. In order for your bird to stand up you will need the four cut ends to be twisted together.

G Tape the four wires together using electrical tape, so that there are no spiky ends and then bend the wires so that they are inside the bird, as far up towards the

head as you can manage. They may need adjusting so that they will stand up easily. If you need your Tweeter to be very stable, cut a small square of thick card and staple your birds feed to it, then it really won't be going anywhere!

Tweet

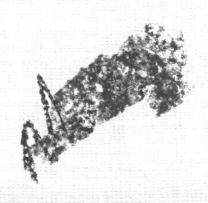

BIRDS WIRE FEET

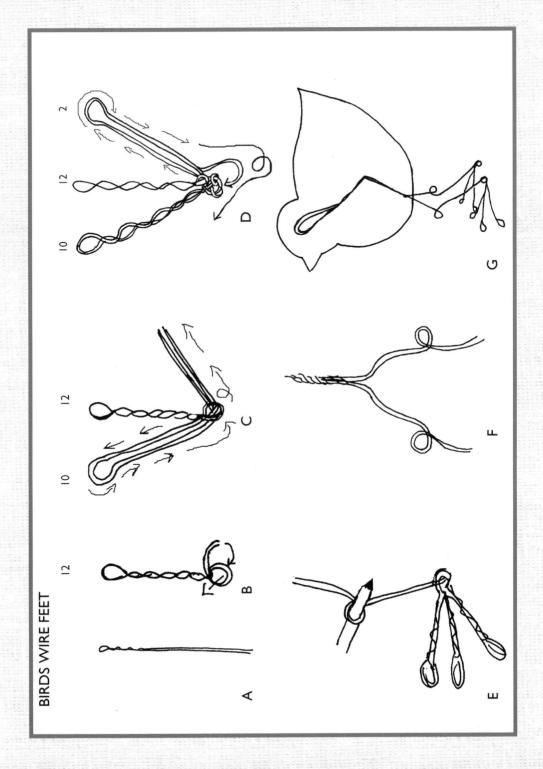

KNITTING BASKET

I adore this technique and again you can add more fabric or less if you want your basket to be higher or lower. The scope for being creative is huge. My basket used around 4 metres of fabric. You can use any combination of colours and just add in new colours as you go or alternative colours to create a striped effect.
I want to make a really big one next!

PLEASE NOTE READ ALL PATTERN INSTRUCTIONS BEFORE STARTING

Finished size
Basket measures - 20cm (8") high, 30cm (12") approx in diameter

Fabric Requirements
This bag uses approx 4m (4 ½ yds) of a selection of dress weight fabrics
1m (1 1/8 yd) of **Fabrics 4, 7, 18,19**
50mm x 3mm Piping cord or sash cord
3 x spools Co-ordinating cotton thread

Cutting List

Cut the fabric on the bias into 2.5cm (1")strips (you can use strips cut on the grain if you prefer but they may fray).

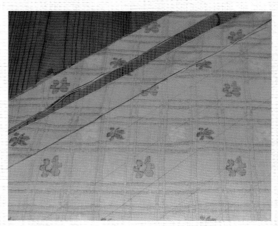

You will also need
Scissors
Rotary cutter
Sewing machine
Hand sewing needle
Bulldog clips

1

2

3

Making Instructions

Step 1 Holding the cord, cover the end with the strip of the fabric. It may help to cut the end of the strip at a 45 degree angle. Begin to wrap the fabric around the cord in a diagonal direction (the grain of the fabric will be in the same direction as the cord)

Step 2 Place the end of the cord under the machine foot to give some tension to the cord whilst wrapping and continue to wrap the fabric around the cord anti-clockwise and angling the fabric so that it wraps evenly around the cord. Wrap about 40cm at a time, then hold with a bulldog clip. Remove from the sewing machine.

Step 3 Fold the end of the wrapped cord over by 2cm. Place the folded end under your machine foot and using a zig zag stitch sew down the centre.

Step 4 When you are close to the end of the shorter piece, lower the needle, raise the foot and pivot the work and wrap the cord to the left. Continue wrapping and sewing to form the base of your bowl or basket.

Step 5 When you are about 10cm away from the bulldog clip, remove the clip and continue to wrap the fabric strip around the cord.

Step 6 If you would like to change your fabric or need to add on a new piece, lower the presser foot to keep your work fixed and place the new fabric under the old one.

Step 7 Keeping your work flat, continue till your work is about 30cm (12") in diameter.

Step 8 Adding height to the sides

Start to lift the base at an angle, keep the palm of your hand under the base of your basket and continue to sew in a spiral. You can change the angle of the sides by holding the base at a steeper or more shallow angle. To achieve vertical sides hold the bowl as close to the machine as you can. Once you have created the corner at the bottom, then hold the base at right angles to the table and work round and round the sides, until you have the desired height.

Step 9 Handles

To create handles make a few reverse stitches and then pull the cord away from the work and sew along the edge of the cord. When you have sewn along the desired length for the handle rejoin the cord making a loop, large enough for your needs and make another reverse stitch.

Make another handle directly opposite.

Continue working another two rounds. You can add further rounds on larger projects.

To finish, cut the cord near a handle and fold the fabric over as if the cord was inside and taper the end neatly to give a smooth join. Sew in place.

On The Fringe Cushion

I had this idea of creating a beautiful fringe that softly melts from one colour into another, for a while, but it did then take me ages to work out how to actually do it! There is a reason most fringes you buy are one colour, it's because it's a lot easier! But I think unusual edges and trims make the difference between an okay cushion and a really stunning one.

PLEASE NOTE READ ALL PATTERN INSTRUCTIONS BEFORE STARTING

Finished Cushion

Cushion measures 56 x 56cm (22" x 22")
SUITABLE FOR USING WITH A SISSIX BIG SHOT

Fabric Requirements

I Fat qtr of **Fabric 5**
1 Fat qtr of **Fabric 6**
1 Fat qtr of **Fabric 17**
Cream Fabric 40 cm (½ yd)
Fabric 13 80 cm (1 yd) of a 44" wide fabric

Cutting Requirements

Fabric 13 cut 2 rectangles 61cm x 35 ¾ cm
(24" x 14") For the cushion back
Fabric 5,6 cut 4 squares of each 4 ½" x 4 ½" or Use Sissix Square 4 ½" x 4 ½" Di 657609
Fabric 13,17 cut 3 squares of each 4 ½" x 4 ½" or Use

Sissix Square
4 ½" x 4 ½" Di 657609

Cream Fabric cut 2 rectangles 61cmx 10cm
(24" x 4") and 2 rectangles
(16 ½" x 4").
Cream Fabric cut 2 squares 4 ½" x 4 ½" or Use Sissix Square 4 ½"x 4 ½" Di 657609

You will also need

For Fringe

Anchor Tapestry Wool from green to red numbers 9200/ 9198/9196/9194/8212/8214/8438/8216/8218 2 skeins of each
Cream Fabric Cut two strips 56cmx 4cm
(23 x 1 ½")
For Cushion
A cushion pad 56cm x 56cm (22 x 22") or fibre filling of your choosing approx a 1 kg bag.
Iron

1

2

1	5	9	13
2	6	10	14
3	7	11	15
4	8	12	16

3

Thick cardboard for cardboard spool for fringe, preferable 3mm (3/16") thick. It needs to be rigid. Cutting knife, board and straight edge
Masking or low tack tape
One can of Stop Fray or similar product or you can just pink the edge using pinking shears

Making & Sewing Instructions

Step 1 Lay out patchwork squares right sides up as in **Pic 1.** Now look at the diagram **Pic 3**, which mirrors the cushion.
Starting top left at square 1 turn this square over on top of square 2 right sides together. Pin top edge. All seams should be ¼" unless otherwise stated.

Match up the pairs of squares in the order as you have done with 1 and 2 for the pairings below.

1 to 2, 3 to 4, 5 to 6, 7 to 8, 9 to 10, 11 to 12, 13 to 14 and 15 to 16.

Stitch all pairs along the pinned edge making sure all edges are matched.

TIP If you have not done patchwork before all seams should be a ¼ ". You will need a 1/4 foot for your machine. Or the easiest way to ensure that the seams are a ¼" is to either adjust the position of your needle if you are able to, so that your line of sewing is always a ¼" in from the edge of your sewing foot. Or place a strip of tape on your machine surface that is a ¼" away from your needle, you can then guide your material along by it.

You can sew one pair of squares after the other as you sew them together, on your machine, without cutting the cotton between the pairs each time. You will end up with a small string of patchwork bunting. Just snip the cotton between each pair when you have reached 15 and 16. The ends will not unravel as they will be sewn into another seam to make your block.

Then iron the seams flat pattern right side up. Lay your pairs out flat in the order of the original pattern in **Pic 1 again,** right sides up. Then do the same again this time turn '1/2' pair of squares' on to '3/4' (right sides together), '5/6' on to '7/8', '9/10' on to '11/12', and finally '13/14' on to '15/16', just joining the pairs this time , along the short top edge, rather than just squares, to create **4 strips, each with 4 squares.**

Iron all seams flat. Lay your 4 strips out this time from left to right, turn Strip'1/2/3/4' on to Strip '5/6/7/8' right sides together, pin and sew left hand long seam. Repeat for other two strips putting '9/10/11/12' on to '13/14/15/16'.

Now you have two blocks of 8. Put them face to face and join the left hand seam where the two cream squares are. Press all seams on the front. You have finished the central block.

Step 2 Take your two shorter cream rectangles. Place Cushion front rightside up on a flat surface and lay strips over the top matching one to the top edge and one to the bottom. Pin and sew ¼" seam. Press.

Step 3 Take your two longer cream rectangles and lie those on your cushion front as with the two shorter pieces but this time along the two remaining sides. Pin a ¼" and sew. Press and trim ends if longer than your block, so that you have a square.

| 9200 | 9198 | 9196 | 9194 | 8212 | 8214 | 8438 | 8216 | 8218 |

4

Step 4 How To Make the Funky Fringe!

For the order of the colours of the Anchor Tapestry Wool from green to red see the list at the start and picture below.

Step 4 Print out the pattern pieces for the cardboard spool that you will wind your wool around to create your lovely funky fringe.

Remember to print out the pattern pieces at 200% which takes them to A4 in size.

Join the three paper sections together and tape, then cut out central rectangle carefully. Place paper pattern piece on thick card, at least 2mm thick, (3/16") such as mount card it needs to be rigid. Draw around it including the inner rectangle. So you have a rectangle within a rectangle. Cut out using straight edge and cutting knife on a cutting board.

* Note be careful when cutting out central rectangle, it must be cut out in one piece, as you then have to rein-sert it back into the place you have cut it out of. When you have done this, tape it with masking tape to hold it in place, using a piece that is just wider than the strip just at each end only and then one small piece across the middle at right angles to your strip to hold the loose rectangle in place in the middle.

Step 5 Spray thin cream strip with Stay Fray or similar product to prevent fraying of edges, place cream strip (23"x 1 ½") centrally, over the inner rectangle, tape it in place down both sides and at each end, so that it is in place with masking or low tack tape. See **Pic 5** Spool Back. Cut the 2 small cuts in the cardboard on your spool edge, as indicated on the paper pattern as these are used to hold your wool ends. Also transfer all markings on your paper pattern to your spool.

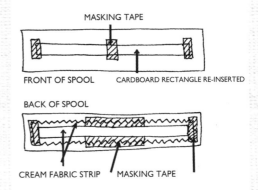

MASKING TAPE

FRONT OF SPOOL   CARDBOARD RECTANGLE RE-INSERTED

BACK OF SPOOL

CREAM FABRIC STRIP   MASKING TAPE

5

Hurray! Now you're ready to wind your wool and make your fringe, which is the fun bit!

6

8

9

10

11

7

12

Step 6 Start with your first colour and secure end of wool in nick or tie around spool once. Taking first colour, wind wool to the next edge marker which indicates when to change colour. **Pic 6** (Note for Eden Warm Heart Cushion change the wool at the WH markers).

Each wool strand should be right up against the next one so that you can't see any cardboard. When joining the next colour simply cut wool just below cream strip then tie a knot so it is as near the centre of the spool as possible.

You can always trim the knots out after if they are visible, so don't worry. Continue to wind the 9 colours down to the end of the inner rectangle in the order:
9200/9198/9196/9194/8212/8214/8438/8216/8218

IMPORTANT TIP *Do not wind wool tightly as it will squeeze cardboard together in the middle making fringe thinner in the middle than at the ends. Make sure that the central cardboard rectangle remains in place while you are winding, it is worth doing this carefully as the end result is great! Secure the end of the last colour in last nick.*

Your spool should now look like this **Pic 7**

Step 7 Now carefully remove the central masking tape strip from the front of your spool, that is securing the cardboard inner rectangle, by parting the wool. **Pic 8**. Then remove the two remaining masking tape strips at each end, holding the inner cardboard rectangle.

Note: Do not remove the masking tape from the other side that has the cream strip on. Remove central cardboard rectangle which is no longer taped by easing it out of one end. **Pic 9**.

Step 8 You then need to reduce your normal stitch size on your machine in order to secure all the strands well. On my machine I put it down to 2, it will vary from machine to machine. Sew the wool to the cream strip right down the centre of the central rectangle, not on to the cardboard though! **Pic 10**

Start by going back and forward a few cms to secure the end. As you go down the channel if there are any gaps where the cream fabric shows through I just cut another bit of wool and laid it down to cover the odd gap. Continue to the end then reverse stitch a few cms again to secure the end.

Step 9 Now for the bit I like the most as it reminds me of making woolly gonks at school when I was little! Using sharp scissors cut all the woollen strands as near to the cardboard edge as possible on each side. Carefully peel off masking tape securing your cream strip to the cardboard. Then sew your fringe twice again down the centre as before but this time parallel with the existing stitching line but a 1/4" either side of it. **Pic 11**.

Step 10 Finally when you have done that and all ends are secure cut down the central line of stitching to create two lengths of fringing. **Pic 12**

Step 11 Repeat **Steps 4-10** again, to make your two other fringe lengths for your cushion. Then trim cream fabric ends and over lap the ends of each fringe by about a 1 cm (½"), joining the same colour to the same colour end of the next section of fringe, stitch together so that you have an even looking fringe. It should now be in one long length.

Step 5 Attaching your Fringe.
As with the Birds Flock Together Cushion, adding the fringe is just like adding piping. So place your pressed Cushion Front face up on flat surface. Start bottom left laying your fringe on your cushion front, fringe ends towards the centre, stitched side parallel to the cushion edge. Pin the start of your fringe and the end first. Then take a moment to make sure all the wool strands are facing inwards and lying in the same direction and at right angles to the cushion edge. You want to avoid stray strands getting caught up in your stitching and spoiling your fringe. Pin the corners and then pin the straight sections. Sew in place along the line of the fringe stitching.

Step 6 Take your two Fabric 13 cushion backs. Turn over a 1cm (¼") and then a 2cm (½") and hem along one of the longer edges on each piece. Place one of the cushion backs reverse side up, on top of your cushion front, matching the longer raw edge to the top of your cushion front, top edge. Place your second back in a similar way but matching up with the front cushion, bottom edge.

Pin all layers together making sure that your pins follow the line of stitching that secured your fringe. This will only be visible on the back so you just have to spend a little time pinning and turning your cushion over to make sure that your pins on the top are matching your stitching on the back. The aim is to sew just as to the left of your fringe stitch line as possible. So that when you turn your cushion right way out you will not see your fringe stitching line. Sew around all sides of the cushion going backwards at the start and finish for a couple of cms to secure the ends. Finish off all raw cut edges as you wish to by over sewing. Turn your cushion inside out. Press. Add cushion pad. Doesn't that look lovely!

Birds Of A Feather
Flock Together Cushion

I love appliqué as it gives me more scope to be creative. So I hope you enjoy making this cushion that is my daughters favorite.

1

Finished Cushion
60cm x 50cm (19 ½"x 23 ½")

Fabric requirements.

Cushion Front - **Cream fabric** 65cm x 55cm (25 ½" x 21 ¾")

For the cream fabric it's best to use the same weight of fabric as you use for the appliqué and preferably a 100% cotton. It will make the appliqué easier.

Cushion Back – Fabric 15 1m (1yd)
Birds - You will only need small amounts of fabrics for the birds so you can always use your own fabric. If you want to make the same birds as on my cushion then you will need the fat quarters below. There will be fabric left over but you will have enough to also make the Tweeter Birds as well.

1 Fat qtr - **Fabric 1**
1 Fat qtr - **Fabric 2**
1 Fat qtr - **Fabric 5**
1 Fat qtr - **Fabric 8 ***
1 Fat qtr - **Fabric 10**
1 Fat qtr - **Fabric 11**
1 Fat qtr - **Fabric 12**
1 Fat qtr - **Fabric 15**

* Only a very small amount of this fabric is used so please feel free to choose another or use fabric to make a Tweeter Bird, see pattern

I Fat qtr of **Freespirit Designer Solid Chocolate S42** for the bird body and crest.
NOTE you will also need a thin strip of the Chocolate fabric for the wires as well but this is longer than a fat qtr so either use a dark brown ribbon approx 65cm x 0.5cm wide (25 ½" x ¼") or buy the minimum quantity you can buy of the chocolate fabric and then you won't need the fat qtr.

Cutting Requirements
Print out or photocopy paper pieces at 100%
Cream Fabric cut a piece 55cm x 65cm (21 ¾" x 25 ½") For Cushion Front
Fabric 15 - Cut 2 pieces 39cm x 65cm (15 ¼" x 25 ½") For Cushion Back - Cut thin strip 4cm x 112cm, width of fabric (1 ½" x 44") and another 4cm x 15cm (1 ½" x 6"). This is for the Piping.
Fabric 21 Chocolate 2 strips 63cm x 0.6cm (24 ¾" x ¼")

Birds
Fabric 1 Cut out 2 Bird B's facing different directions
Fabric 2 Cut out 1 Bird A facing left
Fabric 5 Cut out 1 Bird B facing right
Fabric 8 Cut out 1 Bird Smaller Crest (Please note this can be cut out of one of the other fabrics, as it is such a small piece or use the rest of this fabric to make a Tweeter!)
Fabric 10 Cut out 2 Bird B's facing different directions
Fabric 11 Cut out Bird A wing from right side of fabric
Fabric 12 Cut out Bird A wing from the right side of the fabric
Fabric 15 Cut out 2 Bird C's facing different directions
Freespirit Solid Chocolate Cut Out 2 Bird A's facing each other and 1 Bird's Larger Crest

You will also need;
1 Cushion pad 60cm x 50cm (23 ½" x 19 ¾") or cushion filling of your choice.
Complimentary thread for appliqué. I used Coats duet and chose a lime green, coral and cerise pink, but it's entirely up to you.
Heat and Bond/ Bondaweb or similar fabric to fabric bonding product 50cm x 40cm (19 ¾" x 15 ¾") will be more than enough.
Stitch and Tear paper 2 pieces 20cm x 50cm (8" x 20") each
Piping cord 2.3m (3 yds 7") of 5mm (¼") wide
Anchor embroidery thread cream - 1 skein just for bird's eyes and any other details you may wish to add.

Making & Sewing Instructions
Step 1 Place Bondaweb or similar product sticky face up or rougher side up on a flat surface, lay all wings, birds and crests on top fabric right side up. Pin carefully and cut a Bondaweb shape out for every shape.

Then put a sheet of newspaper with an old sheet or a piece of material over the top, on your ironing board, to prevent your ironing board getting sticky. Turn all wings and heads over so that the sticky side of the Bondaweb is face down on top of the wrong side of your material, and iron in place. Peel off all backings.
Step 2 Lay cream fabric piece down on a flat surface, measure up the shorter sides and mark with a pin at 15cm and 33cm (6" and 13"). Then either stick Bondaweb to each strip of Chocolate fabric or the ribbon of your choice, in the same way as you did for the birds. Lay fabric or ribbon the length of the cushion from pin to pin. Iron on and then stitch in place to form the wires. Position birds on your wires, refer to picture **Pic 1**, tucking the crests behind the heads of the Bird A's. Iron all bird bodies and wings and crests in place.
Step 3. Turn the cushion front over to the wrong side and iron on 'Stitch and Tear' rectangles to cover your two lines of birds. This supports the cream fabric as you are appliquéing it and prevents it puckering. I learnt this by doing it the wrong way first! It is worth doing.
Step 4 You can either hand appliqué the birds or machine stitch them depending on whether you have a machine that will do satin stitch or over sew them by hand. If you wish to machine stitch alter the foot on your machine to one that will accommodate satin stitch and have a practice before you do your cushion if you have not done it before. Refer to **Pic 1&2** on 'Edenville Cottages'. Particularly practise sewing around corners. There is a knack to it, which involves making sure you are on the right side of the stitch when you turn the fabric to go around a corner.
I used contrasting cottons on each bird as you can see in the picture. I also did some extra detailing on the crests as I wanted to make them a feature. **Pic 3**
Use embroidery thread to create eyes on birds by doing a

few over stitches or a French Knot, again be creative it could just be a cross stitch. I like to leave something's up to you! It is entirely your decision how much detail you wish to add. After you have appliquéd remove the stitch and tear from the reverse side.

3

Step 6 Piping
 Join your two thin strips of Fabric 15 together, by matching the short ends together with the fabrics right sides together. Stitch a 1cm or 3/8" seam and press flat.

Then put the wrong sides together and match long edges, press to form a crease as a guide to where your chord should lie. Open long strip and lay your piping along the length of it, in the fold you have just created down the middle. Fold the long edges back over to meet each other and tack the chord in place, as near to the chord as possible, to hold it in the centre of the strip. Lay your cushion front on a flat surface, right side up. Pin and then tack your piping tube to the edge of your cushion, leaving an extra 3cm or 1" spare at the start and end. Tack as close to your existing line of tacking on your piping tube as possible, with the piping fold side always towards the centre of the cushion and cut edges of your tube matching the edges

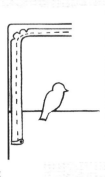

4

of the cushion front. As you go around the corner you will need to cut the two edges of your piping tube at right angles to your tube but not cut the tacking, to ease it around the corner. See **Pic 4**. Where the ends meet open the tube ends. Cut each chord so that they meet perfectly. Cut fabric ends so that they overlap each other by approx 3cm or 1". Turn back fabric ends under by 1.5cm or ½",
overlap and pin and tack to end. See **Pic 5**
Step 6 Take your two Fabric 15 backs. Turn over a ¼"

and then a ½" and hem along one of the longer edges on each piece. Turn your cushion front right side up on a flat surface, place one of the cushion backs wrong side up on top matching the longer raw edge to the top

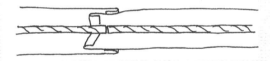

5

of your cushion front top edge. Place your second back in a similar way but matching up with the longer bottom edge at the bottom. See **Pic 6**.

Pin all layers together making sure that you pin as close to your piping tacking line as possible. This will only be visible on the back, so you just have to spend

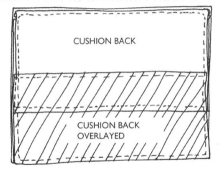

CUSHION BACK

CUSHION BACK
OVERLAYED

6

a little time pinning through the top but turning your cushion over to make sure that your pins on the top are matching your tacking line of your piping on the back. The aim is to sew as close to your piping as possible. Alter your machine foot so that your needle is to the left of the foot edge as you look at it, this ensures that your sewing line is as close to the piping edge as possible and sandwiched between the top and bottom layers of fabric. Sew around all sides of the cushion going backwards at the start and finish for a couple of centimetres to secure the ends. Finish off all raw cut edges as you wish to by over sewing. Remove tacking. Press.

Turn inside out and add cushion pad.

EDEN SUMMER QUILT

Finished Size

Quilt is approximately 56" x 63"

Fabric Requirements

Quantity quoted for using both a rotary cutter or a Sissix machine.

Please note Fabric quantity does not including binding and backing fabric.

For cutting chart see page xx

Cutting Instructions

This quilt has been made using Sizzix quilt dies

2 ½" square die 657607 (2" when finished)
4 ½" square die 657609 (4" when finished)
4½" triangle die 657613 (4" when finished)

Please Note - If you do not have the Sizzix machine then fabric can be cut using rotary equipment or scissors. The cutting instructions are different so please be sure to use the appropriate ones.

Using Sizzix machine:

Using die 657607 square cut 2 ½" squares as follows:
90 squares from fabric 15
90 squares from fabric 1
60 squares from fabric 5

Using die 657609 cut 4 ½" squares as follows:
73 squares from fabric 22
9   squares from fabric 14
10 squares from fabric 2
9   squares from fabric 17
8   squares from fabric 6

Using die 657613 cut 4½" triangles as follows:
10 triangles from fabric 2
20 triangles from fabric 5
24 triangles from fabric 6
21 triangles from fabric 8
2   triangles from fabric 14
2   triangles from fabric 17
47 triangles from fabric 22

If you are using rotary cutting equipment or scissors then cut as follows:
90 squares 2½" from fabric 15
90 squares 2½" from fabric 1
60 squares 2½" from fabric 5

73 squares 4½" from fabric 22
9   squares 4½" from fabric 14
10 squares 4½" from fabric 2
9   squares 4½" from fabric 17
8 squares 4½" from fabric 6

Cut 10 squares 4 7/8" from fabric 5 and then cut into 20 triangles
Cut 12 squares 4 7/8" from fabric 6 and then cut into 24 triangles
Cut 11 squares 4 7/8" from fabric 8 and then cut into 22 triangles (only need 21)
Cut 5 squares 4 7/8" from fabric 2 and then cut into 10 triangles
Cut 1 squares 4 7/8" from fabric 14 and then cut into 2 triangles
Cut 1 squares 4 7/8" from fabric 17 and then cut into 2 triangles
Cut 24 squares 4 7/8" from fabric 22 and then cut into 48 triangles (only need 47)

1

2

Making and sewing instructions

All seams are ¼" and seams should be pressed to one side, not open. This quilt is mainly constructed using four or sixteen patch blocks. The blocks when completed, but before assembly, should measure 8.5" x 8.5".

Refer to Pic 2 throughout the construction stage and when putting the blocks together. It will assist in layout and in fabric identification.

The blocks are constructed using squares stitched together (some squares may initially be made from 2 triangles) in rows. To match your seams accurately press the seams of the rows in opposite directions, then when you stitch the rows together pin together at each seam. This is referred to as pin matching.

Make all your blocks before assembling the quilt top.

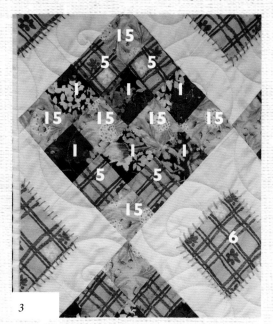

3

Pic 3 16 Patch block
16 patch blocks rows– you will need 15 of these

Lay out your 16 squares and stitch into 4 rows of 4 and then stitch the 4 rows together.

**4 patch blocks for appliqué – you will need 8 of these blocks

Lay out 4 fabric 22 4.5" squares and stitch into 2 rows of 2 and then sew the 2 rows together to form a 4 patch block

Note: The appliqué 'patches' will be added to these blocks when your quilt top is assembled.

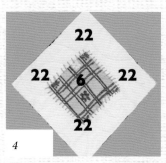

4

Set 1 – you will need 4 of these

Take 3 4.5" squares of fabric 22 and 1 of fabric 17 and stitch into 2 rows of 2 and then stitch 2 rows together

5

Set 2 - you will need 5 of these

Lay out 2 4.5" squares of fabric 2 and 1 of fabric 17 and 1 of fabric 14 and stitch together in 2 rows. Then stitch the 2 rows together.

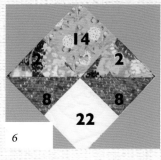

6

Set 3 – you will need 4 of these

Take 2 triangles of fabric 2 and 2 of fabric 8, join these carefully along the bias edge to form a square and press without stretching the fabric. Make 2 squares.
Take 1 of these squares and stitch a 4.5" square of fabric 22 to the right hand side.
Take the other and stitch a 4.5" square of fabric 14 to right hand side of it.
Now stitch the 2 rows together to form a four patch

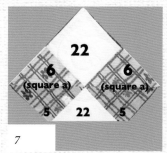

7

Set 4 – you will need 5 of these - NB these blocks are not a complete square when made up as they are at the edge of the quilt.

Take 1 triangle of fabric 5 and 1 of fabric 6, join these carefully along the bias edge to form a square and press without stretching the fabric. Repeat this so you have 2 squares when stitched together (square a).

Take a 4.5" square of fabric 22 and stitch it to the left of one of these squares

Take a triangle of fabric 22 and stitch it to the right of the other (square a).
Stitch the 2 rows together – the small triangle should be at the bottom of the finished block.

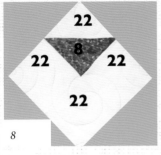

8

Set 5 – you will need 4 of these

Take 1 small triangle of fabric 22 and 1 triangle of fabric 8, join these carefully along the bias edge to form a square and press without stretching the fabric. Stitch a 4.5" cream square to the right of this square. Take 2 4.5" squares of fabric 22 and stitch together.
Stitch the 2 rows together to form a four patch.

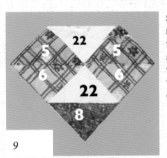

9

Set 6 – you will need 5 of these – NB these blocks are not a complete square when made up as they are at the edge of the quilt.

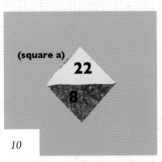

(square a)

10

Take 1 small triangle of fabric 22 and 1 triangle of fabric 8, join these carefully along the bias edge to form a square and press without stretching the fabric (square a).

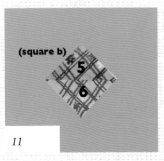

(square b)

11

Take 1 triangle of fabric 5 and 1 of fabric 6, join these carefully along the bias edge to form a square and press without stretching the fabric (square b), repeat this so you have 2 squares.

Stitch 1 of the (squares b's) to the left of (square a's). Stitch the other (square b) to the right of a triangle of fabric 22.

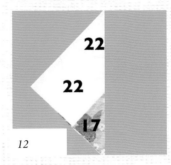

12

Set 7 you will need 1 of these

Take triangle of fabric 22, triangle of fabric 17 and a 4" square of fabric 22. Stitch the triangle of fabric 22 to the top of the square of fabric 22 and stitch the triangle of fabric 17 to the right of the square.

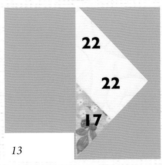

13

Set 8 you will need 1 of these

Take triangle of fabric 22, triangle of fabric 17 and a 4" square of fabric 22.
Stitch the triangle of fabric 22 to the top of the square of fabric 22 and stitch the triangle of fabric 17 to the left of the square.

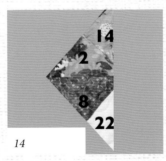

14

Set 9 you will need 1 of these

Take a triangle each of fabric 2 and fabric 8 and stitch together to form a square. Then stitch a triangle of fabric 22 to the right of this square and a triangle of fabric 14 to the top.

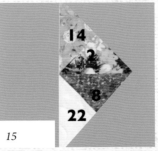

15

Set 10 you will need 1 of these

Take a triangle each of fabric 2 and fabric 8 and stitch together to form a square. Then stitch a triangle of fabric 22 to the left of this square and a triangle of fabric 14 to the top.

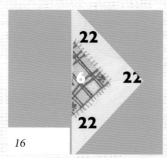

16

Set 11 you will need 4 of these
Take a square of fabric 22 and 2 triangles of fabric 22, stitch a triangle to the top and the left of the square. These will have appliqué triangles of fabric 6 added after assembly of your quilt top.

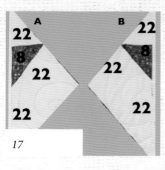

17

Set 12 you will need 1 of each of these
A Take a square of fabric 22, 2 triangles of fabric 22 and a triangle of fabric 8. Stitch the triangle of fabric 22 to the left of the square and stitch the triangle of fabric 8 to the top then stitch the other triangle of fabric 22 to fabric 8. These blocks will need trimming to fit when assembling the quilt top.
B Take a square of fabric 22, 2 triangles of fabric 22 and a triangle of fabric 8. Stitch the triangle of fabric 22 to the right of the square and stitch the triangle of fabric 8 to the top, then stitch the other triangle of fabric 22 to fabric 8.

Constructing your top

Lay out your blocks to correspond with the picture, in diagonal rows and stitch. You will have 10 rows.

Stitch the 10 rows together.

Now take 18 triangles of fabric 22 and stitch them into the gaps at the top and bottom.

Take 4 triangles of fabric 22 and add them to the outer corners – you will need to trim these when stitched on to square up the edges.

Applique – take 8 squares of fabric 6 turn under a ¼" press. Stitch to the centre of the blocks of fabric 22 made at **. Use a blanket stitch to appliqué to give a naïve look to your quilt or just stitch as in picture.
Take 4 triangles of fabric 8 and appliqué them, as in main picture of quilt, to the four large inset triangles of fabric 22.

Completing your quilt

To complete your quilt you will need wadding and backing of your choice.

Layer up and pin or baste to secure.

Quilt as desired by hand or machine.

Add your binding to finish your quilt – don't forget to add a label to the back.

EDEN BUNTING

This project is great to make for parties or just for decoration. You can make your chain as long or as short as you like and can also connect the flowers to make a curtain or triangular shaped hanging. I used my wonderful Sizzix Bigshot (die cutting machine) to make it. It has taken all the angst out of cutting things accurately for me, which to be honest stopped me making a lot of things as I know I am not great at cutting things out really accurately particularly since developing a frozen shoulder after an injury.

PLEASE NOTE READ ALL PATTERN INSTRUCTIONS BEFORE STARTING
SUITABLE FOR USING WITH A SIZZIX BIG SHOT
You will need Die 658105 or if you do not have a Sizzix Machine then use the Leaf and Leaf Centre Template, at the back of the book. Enlarge by 200%.

Finished Size
Eden Daisy Bunting measures – 1 flower 15cm x 15cm (6" x 6") Eight flowers gives you a string of 1.2m (47") Eden Hidden Circle Bunting - Seven flowers gives you 1m (39 ½")

Fabric Requirements
Really I would suggest using up any scraps you have. I have used Eden fabric of course for my bunting! You can see which patterns I have used from the key at the front. But as they are such small bits of fabric I am not going to quote quantities.

Cutting List
For two flowers
Cut out 8 fabric leaves, 4 in each fabric, using your Sizzix Die 658105, lay the fabric just over the two larger leaves as you don't want to waste fabric cutting out the smaller ones as well. You can cut up to 8 layers of fabric at a time

(that makes me very happy!). If you don't have a Sizzix then copy the leaf at the back of the book and cut it out of paper as a template.
Cut out – 8 Fabric to fabric bonding leaves
Cut out – 2 Flower Centres (see template at the back of the book)

You will also need
Interfacing - Pelmet weight
Fabric to fabric bonding paper, such as Heat & Bond or Bondaweb - heavier weight
Sharp scissors
Hole punch
Wool and Thick Cotton or embroidery thread, for joining leaves together
Iron/ Ironing board and old tea towel

Making Instructions
Step 1 Please note *These are the basic instructions for making two flowers which will enable you to make the Eden Bunting as all you then need to do is repeat these instructions over and over depending on how long you want your bunting to be. You could also make the Bunting Flowers larger by increasing the size of the leaf template and flower centre.*
Place your old tea towel or piece of fabric on your ironing

board, this is just to stop your ironing board getting sticky which no one needs! Place all fabric leaves right side down with a matching fabric bonding leaf on top, non-sticky side up. Iron in place. Peel off backings. Position all leaves on your piece of interfacing and iron on. Cut out leaves. You could cut out your interfacing leaves on your Sissix too, but it would probably take more time as you can't fold it as easily and would waste interfacing. But it's up to you.

Step 2 Take each leaf and punch a hole carefully in each end of your leaf. **Pic 1**. Punch two holes side by side in your flower centres. Then thread a woollen strand (approx 15cm (6") long) through each of the holes of the flower centre, then thread one end through the holes of two leaves, fabric side up and the other end through the end holes of the other two leaves. Cross the wool over and go back through the opposite holes and back to the flower front. Cross over and go back down the first

hole you went down with each strand. **Pic 2**. You should now have four leaves joined to one flower centre, two leaves to each side. Cross the wool over behind your flower, come back up through the opposite hole in your flower centre, cross over and back down the other hole again. Like sewing a large button on. Now tie your ends off behind your flower tightly by doing a reef knot. All that means is tie a knot by doing the left strand over the right and then right over left, then the knot won't slip. I can hear my Guide Captain saying those words even now! **Pic 3**

Step 3 Repeat for your other flower. Then you should have a completed flower. Then there are several options of how to join them together. I have shown two options in the **Pic 1**. For The Hidden Circle Bunting I joined two leaves together so you don't need wool at the top. **Pic 4**. For the Daisy Chain Bunting I only attached one leaf of each flower to the next leaf and then threaded wool through the top petal. **Pic 5** see also **Pic 6**. You can also attach additional rows together below each flower on Daisy Chain Bunting. The possibilities are endless!

Tip The bunting can look very different depending on what background you put it on. Here it is on blue, so that is something to bear in mind when you are working out where you would like to hang it. Remember what colour you put next to anything effects how all the colours look together.

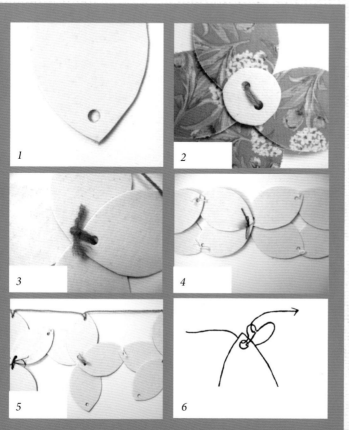

1

2

3

4

5

6

PATCH BAG

This is a really lovely sized bag not to big and not too small. It has a great drawstring top for easy access. You can also add more patches if you wish but this time around I thought it was nice to keep it simple. It works really well for every day as well as for the summer. I hope you enjoy it!

PLEASE NOTE READ ALL PATTERN INSTRUCTIONS BEFORE STARTING

Finished Size

Bag measures: 27cm (10 5/8") high, 40cm (15 ¾") seam to seam, 29cm (11 3/8") wide at base, 12cm (4 ¾") deep. Handles: 19cm (7 1/2") drop

Fabric Requirements

½ m (20") **Fabric 21** ½ m (20") for **Main Fabric** of bag

1m (30") **Fabric 12** for **Main Body Lining** for interior of bag, handles, drawstring top and patches.

20cm (8") **Fabric 11** for patches.

Additional Requirements

1/2m (20") Thermolam© Vilene Compressed Fleece batting
1/2m (20") 2oz polyester wadding,
2 m (80") 1.5cm (½") ribbon, embroidery thread, machine thread.

Cutting list

Main Body. Cut rectangles 44cm by 36cm (17 3/8" x 14 ¼") Cut two rectangles for **Main Body** pieces in **Fabric 21**, two in **Main Body Lining Fabric 12**, two in Thermolam fleece and two in 2oz polyester wadding.

Handles. Cut rectangle 16cm by 46cm (6 3/8" x 18 1/8"). Cut two handles in Fabric 12, and two in Thermolam fleece.

Drawstring top. Rectangle 44cm by 34cm. Cut one in Fabric 12.

Patches. Square 7cm by 7cm. (3'x3") Cut 8 in **Fabric 11** and 8 in **Fabric 12**

Ribbon. Cut two lengths of 96cm (38")

Pattern notes

All seam allowances are 1cm unless otherwise stated.

Step 1. Bag Body Patches.
Apply the Thermolam interfacing to both pieces of the **Main Body** Pieces (**Fabric 21**) using spray baste or temporary fabric adhesive. With the right sides up

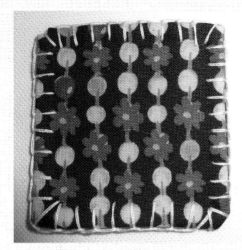

measure 12cm (4 ¾") from the top. Draw a straight line along this point from side to side on both pieces. Match up the same fabric patches right sides together. Using a 0.5cm (¼") seam, stitch around the square leaving a small gap in the bottom seam for turning. Clip the corners and carefully turn out the squares pushing the fabric from the gap inside. Press. Using a toning embroidery thread, blanket stitch around all the squares.

Using spray baste lay the squares centrally along the line you drew on the bag body. Match the corner points to the line and place each square against the next one. Pin the patches. Using a machine thread the same colour as your embroidery thread, stitch each patch into place as close to the edge of the patch as possible.

Step 3. **Corners**.
Press the lining seams flat. Take one corner and push together so that the bottom seam and the side seam are on top of each other. Draw a line 6cm (2 3/8") from the corner. Stitch along the line.

Repeat with the other corner. Trim the corner. Repeat for the main fabric. Turn the main fabric to the right side and push the corners out.

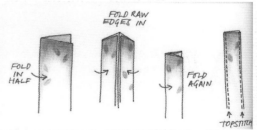

Step 2. **Completing the bag body**.
Using spray baste or pins, secure the polyester wadding to the wrong side of the bag body pieces. Place the bag body pieces right sides together and stitch along both sides and the bottom. Repeat for the lining fabric but leave a gap in the bottom seam for turning.

Step 4. **Handles.**
Apply the Thermolam interfacing to the fabric. Fold both sides to the centre and press. Fold raw edges into the centre and fold over again. Topstitch down both sides.

Mark the centre top of the main fabric on both the front

and the back. On either side of the centre mark measure 7cm (2 ¾ ") and mark. Stitch the handle ends at these marks.

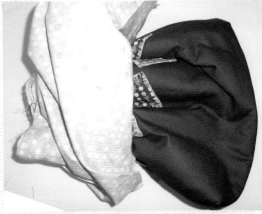

Step 5. Drawstring Top.

Turn the outside edges at the sides under by 1cm (3/8") and press. Make the casing on both pieces of the drawstring top by turning under the top seam by 1cm (3/8") and turning again by 2cms (3/4") Press. Stitch close the turned edge, triple stitch at each end to secure. Place the pieces right sides together and stitch up both sides along the 1cm crease. Stop 4.5cm from the casing. Press the seam flat.

that the ties are at either ends of the casing. Pull the ribbon to gather up the casing.

Step 5. **Finish.** Give the bag a final press. If a dirt resist finish is required spray the bag with stain resistant spray.

Step 6. Assembling the Body.

Slip the drawstring top over the bag body, right sides together, so that the raw edge of the drawstring top and the top of the bag are together. Stitch around the top of the bag using a 1 cm (3/8")seam.

Then slip the main body inside the lining fabric. Match the side seams and pin around the top. Stitch around the top through all layers, triple stitching over the handles. Turn to the right side through the gap in the lining. Stitch the gap closed.

Step 7. Inserting the Ribbon.

Using a pin insert a length of ribbon through both sides of the casing and tie. Repeat for the other length of ribbon but start inserting from the opposite end so

EDENVILLE COTTAGES

I just love these little doorstops they are fun and almost look like a little village. They have a zip so you can take out the filling and wash them too!

PLEASE NOTE READ ALL PATTERN INSTRUCTIONS BEFORE STARTING

Finished Size
28cms (11") high, 33cms (13") wide and 8cms (3.25") deep

Fabric Requirements
'Green Gables' Cottage
Refer to Fabric Key at the front of the book.
Fat qtr of **Fabric 2** for ROOF
Fat qtr of **Fabric 9** for DOOR and WINDOWS
Fat qtr of **Fabric 10** for HOUSE WALL
'Cherry Cottage' Cottage
Refer to Fabric Key at the front of the book.
Fat qtr of **Fabric 18** for ROOF
Fat qtr of **Fabric 8** for DOOR and WINDOWS
Fat qtr of **Fabric 12** for HOUSE WALL

You will also need
30cm (12") fabric to fabric bonding (Bondaweb, Heat and Bond or similar)
Stitch and Tear piece Size 15.5cm x20cm (10 x8")
Contrasting thread for appliqué
Button for door handle
Small bag of toy wadding

1 kg bag of rice for each cottage
34cm (13 ½") Zip

Cutting list
For each cottage cut the following. You don't need templates as they are all rectangles
House Bottom / Walls (Cut 2) 35.5cm x19cm (14" x 7 ½")
Windows (Cut 4) 6.5cm x 6.5cm (2 ½" x 2 ½")
Door (Cut 2) 6.5cm x 9cm (2 ½" x 3")
Chimney (Cut 1) 12.75cm x 12.75cm (5'x5")
Roof (Cut 2) 35.5cm x 20.4cm 14" by 8"
Cut the shape following these measurements: Bottom of roof 14" (35.5cms). Measure 2" (5cm) up both sides from the bottom and mark. Measure 8" (20.4cms) centrally across the top of the roof and mark both ends of the 8". Draw a 6" (15.3cms) angled line from the 8" marks to the 2" marks on both sides.

Cut fabric bonding to match the doors and windows sizes.
Stitch and Tear (Cut 2) 15.5cm by 10 cms (10" by 4")
All seam allowances are 1cm (3/8") unless otherwise stated.

Step 1 Place all the material door and window shapes on ironing board wrong side up. Match fabric bonding shapes right side up over each fabric shape. Place spare bit of old fabric or tea towel over both layers. Iron as instructed by bonding material manufacturer.
Please note *Be careful not to cut the fabric bonding shapes larger than your material shapes as otherwise you will make your ironing board sticky!*

Step 2 Peel the paper backing from the fabric bonding. Take one of the wall pieces and fold in half. Press. Measure 5cm (2") from the bottom of the wall piece and mark. Take one door piece and fold in half long-ways. Place

the door piece right side up so that the bottom of door matches the mark and the fold on the door matches the fold on the wall. Iron into place. Position windows either side quite close to door but leave enough distance from cut edge above door. Iron windows in place. Repeat for the other wall.

Step 3 All doors should now be in position and stuck to your fabric. Iron stitch and tear two rectangles to wrong side of fabric over the windows and doors.
Set machine to narrow zig-zag to enable satin stitch. Satin stitch using contrasting thread around the window and door fabric. **Pic 1**. Add a cross for windows and letterbox shape as in **Pic 2**. The curtains can be whatever shape you like. If you do not have zig-zag on your machine you can use straight stitch or hand sew them on which looks just as nice.

Step 4 Sew on button door handle. **Pic 3**

Step 5 Take chimney piece and fold each longer edge into the middle of the strip and then fold two folded edges together. Iron. Fold in half matching two shortest ends together. Iron. Stitch down both sides of the chimney close to the edges.

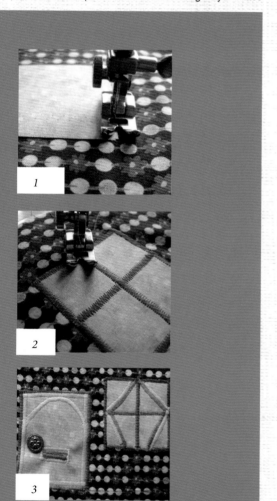

1

2

3

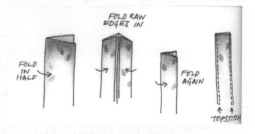

FOLD RAW
EDGES IN

FOLD
IN
HALF

FOLD
AGAIN

TOPSTITCH

Step 6 Place the house front bottom and the house front roof right sides together and stitch together to form a central 2.5cm (1") seam. Lay the 34cm (13 ½") zip right side up next to the house back bottom and house back roof.

Step 7 Fold the roof straight edge over by 1.2cm (½") and stitch along the top edge of the zip quite close to the teeth. Fold the house back bottom over

by 3cms (1.2 inches) and stitch to the bottom edge of the zip so that the folded edge covers the teeth.

Topstitch from the edges of the house to the zip stop at one end and the zip pull at the other end.

Step 8 Fold the chimney in half and place 17.8cms (7") from the right hand edge on the right side of the fabric. Make sure both cut edges of the chimney and the top of the roof are parallel. Stitch across the chimney close to the edge. OPEN THE ZIP. Place the house front and house back pieces right sides together. Stitch completely around the edges. Press.

Step 9 To make the flat bottom, reach through the zip opening and grab the bottom corners of the house. Fold one bottom corner flat matching up the centre bottom seam with the centre side seam, right sides together. Measure 8.2cm (3 ¼") from the corner along the seam line and mark.

Draw a straight line at this mark. Double stitch along the line. Repeat for the other corner.

Turn the housethe right side out.

Step 10 To finish, fill the bottom half with rice and stuff the roof space with toy wadding. You can tip the rice straight into the house or use a rice bag. Zip it up and enjoy your Edenville Cottage!

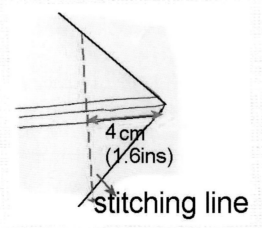

4 cm
(1.6ins)

stitching line

Warm Heart
Cushion

I wanted this to be an eye catching feature cushion, for a bed or a nice seat. I also thought it might be nice to give as a gift with an extra heart pocket in the middle that you could put a note in. I might give it to my daughter Polly when she goes to University with a note in it as she has already baggsied the Eden quilt for her bed.
Yes, I know I'm a bit of a softy.

1

2

Finished Cushion 43cm x 35cm (17" x 14") including fringe

Fabric Requirements
½ m (½ yd) of Fabric 10
Cream Fabric 40cm (½ yd)

Cutting Requirements

Print out the Heart Warming Cushion pattern pieces enlarging them by 200%. Join the two Larger Heart Pieces together at the markers
Cut out 1 Large Heart in Fabric 10 by folding over your fabric wrong sides together and placing the heart paper piece to the fold.
Repeat for Small Heart using Fabric 10
Cut out 1 Large Heart in the Cream fabric of your choice

For Fringe
Anchor Tapestry Wool from green to red numbers 9200/9198/9196/9194/8212/8214/8438/8216/8218
1 skein of each
Or wool of your own choosing equivalent to the length of a tapestry wool skein.
Cream Fabric Cut two strips 56cm x 4cm
(23 x 1 ½")

You will also need

Cushion filling of your choosing only about 300gm
Iron
70cm x 15cm (28" x 6") Piece of 3mm (1/8") thick
cardboard, to cut out your cardboard spool, which is
66cm x 10cm (26"x 4") when cut out.

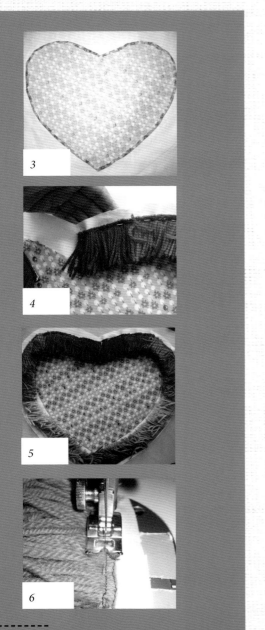

3

4

5

6

Cutting knife, board and straight edge
Masking or low tack tape
One can of Stop Fray OR similar product OR you can just
pink the edge using pinking shears

Making & Sewing Instructions

Step 1 With your smaller green heart face down turn over
a ¼" seam around the edge and press with your iron.
Pic 3 At the top of your heart make a little snip with
your scissors in order to turn the fabric over, where the
two halves of the heart meet. Place this smaller heart
centrally on top of your Cream Large Heart. Pin it and
then hand sew it or machine sew it to your Cream Heart.

Step 2 Make your Funky Fringe by following Steps 4 -10
in the On The Fringe Cushion pattern.

Step 3 Place your green Larger Heart Cream piece (with
the smaller heart attached) right side up on a flat surface.
Pin one of your fringe lengths, starting with the red end, at
the centre top of your heart, ½" in. The fringe side should
point towards the centre of the cushion, the fringe sewn
edge side should be parallel to the cream heart cut edge.
Pic 4. Pin each end of the fringe first at the centre top of
your heart and the bottom centre point, 1cm (½") past
the point at the bottom and top. As everyone's fringe will
vary slightly just take a little time straightening out your
fringe and easing it around the edge making sure that it is
equidistant from the green heart in the middle.
Please note It is important that your fringe ends overlap a
little at the top and bottom so that you don't end up with a
gap when you turn it inside out eventually.

As each person's fringe will vary slightly it doesn't matter
if you end up coming a little further in with your fringe it's
more important not to have a gap. Stitch an extra few
strands over the cream ends if you think you will see
them if your fringes are a bit thin at the ends. Pin the rest
of your fringe to your heart. **Pic 5.**
Tack if you wish or if you are confident enough, to do so,
just sew in place just to the left of your fringe stitching line
see **Pic 6.**

Step 4 Make sure all your fringe is straight and not
caught up again.
Place Large Green Heart on top of your cream heart

face down. Pin with just four pins top and bottom and side to side to hold in place. Turn your cushion over carefully so as not to disturb the fringe. Pin along the fringe sewing line you have just made. Take out the four pins on the other side. Sew exactly along this line leaving a 10cm (4") gap to turn your cushion inside out. Snip carefully around the curved edge of your cushion, at right angles to your seam, at intervals of about an inch. Not too close to the seam, just enough to make a nice curved seam when turning your cushion inside out.

Step 5 Stuff your cushion with your desired filling. Turning remaining seams of your 4" gap under and over sewing to close hole.

Join My Cat Club
Chance to Win FREE Goodies every month!

nel
ART FOR LIVING
www.nelpatterns.com

The Cat Club   Happy Cat   Benny & Blossom   Kitty and Cat   Dotty Cat

With every fabric collection I design there is a Cat Pattern for you to make to go with it. They are like little mascots for each collection.

All you have to do is go to my website **www.nelpatterns.com** and register for the Cat Club which is FREE, then you automatically get:

* *The Happy Cat doorstop pattern as a FREE download & Kitty & Cat Cushion.*

* *The chance to win the monthly FREE GIVEAWAY*

* *And I'll then let you know when the next cat pattern is out along with news of my next fabric collection.*

Happy Cat from Happy Go Lucky FREE DOWNLOAD

Dotty Cat from Katharine's Wheel

Kitty and Cat Cushion FREE DOWNLOAD

NEW Benny and Blossom the new Eden Cats

Whats Coming next...

nel ART FOR LIVING *Secret Garden* FreeSpirit *Denim Colourway*

nelpatterns.com

Stockists List

AUSTRALIA: Australian Country Spinners, Pty Ltd, Level 7, 409 St. Kilda Road, Melbourne Vic 3004.
Tel: 03 9380 3830
Email: sales@auspinners.com.au

AUSTRIA: Coats Harlander GmbH, Autokaderstrasse 31, A -1210 Wien. Tel: (01) 27716 – 0

BELGIUM: Coats Benelux, Ring Oost 14A, Ninove, 9400, Belgium Tel: 0346 35 37 00
Email: sales.coatsninove@coats.com

CANADA: Westminster Fibers Inc, 8 Shelter Drive, Greer South Carolina, NH03060 Tel: 800 445-9276
Email: rowan@westminsterfibers.com

CHINA: Coats Shanghai Ltd, No 9 Building , Baosheng Road, Songjiang Industrial Zone, Shanghai.
Tel: (86- 21) 5774 3733 Email: victor.li@coats.com

DENMARK: Coats Danmark A/S, Nannasgade 28, 2200 Kobenhavn N Tel: (45) 35 86 90 50
Fax: (45) 35 82 15 10 Email: info@hpgruppen.dk Web: www.hpgruppen.dk

FINLAND: Coats Opti Oy, Ketjutie 3, 04220 Kerava
Tel: (358) 9 274 871

FRANCE: Coats France / Steiner Frères, SAS 100, avenue du Général de Gaulle, 18 500 Mehun-Sur-Yèvre Tel: (33) 02 48 23 12 30
Web: www.coatscrafts.fr

GERMANY: Coats GmbH, Kaiserstrasse 1, D-79341 Kenzingen Tel: (49) 7644 8020
Web: www.coatsgmbh.de

HOLLAND: Coats Benelux, Ring Oost 14A, Ninove, 9400, Belgium Tel: 0346 35 37 00
Email: sales.coatsninove@coats.com

HONG KONG: Coats Shanghai Ltd, No 8 Building, Export & Processing Garden, Songjiang Industrial Zone, Shanghai.
Tel: (86- 21) 5774 3733-326
Email: victor.li@coats.com

ICELAND: Storkurinn, Laugavegi 59, 101 Reykjavik
Tel: (354) 551 8258 Email: storkurinn@simnet.is

ISRAEL: Beit Hasidkit, Sokolov St No2, 44256 Kfar Sava Tel: (972) 97482381

ITALY: Coats Cucirini s.r.l., Via Sarca 223, 20126 Milano Tel: 800 992377
Email: servizio.clienti@coats.com

KOREA: Coats Korea Co Ltd, 5F Eyeon B/D, 935-40 Bangbae- Dong, Seocho-Gu, Seoul Tel: (82) 2 521 6262.
Web: www.coatskorea.co.kr

LEBANON: y.knot, Saifi Village, Mkhalissiya Street 162, Beirut
Tel: (961) 1 992211 Email: y.knot@cyberia.net.lb

LUXEMBOURG: Bastel Kiste, Rue Du Fort Elizabeth 17-19, 1463 Luxemburg Tel: 00352 40 05 06

MALTA: John Gregory Ltd, 8 Ta'Xbiex Sea Front, Msida MSD 1512, Malta
Tel: +356 2133 0202, Email: raygreg@onvol.net

NEW ZEALAND: ACS New Zealand, 1 March Place, Belfast, Christchurch. Tel: 64-3-323-6665

NORWAY: Coats Knappehuset AS, Pb 100 Ulset, 5873 Bergen. Tel: (47) 55 53 93 00

SINGAPORE: Golden Dragon Store, 101 Upper Cross Street #02-51, People's Park Centre, Singapore 058357. Tel: (65) 6 5358454
Email: gdscraft@hotmail.com

SOUTH AFRICA: Arthur Bales LTD, 62 4th Avenue, Linden 2195 Tel: (27) 11 888 2401
Email: arthurb@new.co.za

SPAIN: Coats Fabra, Santa Adria 20, 08030 Barcelona Tel: 932908400
Email: atencion.clientes@coats.com

SWEDEN: Coats Expotex AB, Division Craft, JA Wettergrensgatta 7, Vastra Frolunda, 431 30 Goteburg Goteborg Tel: (46) 33 720 79 00

SWITZERLAND: Coats Stroppel AG, CH -5300 Turgi (AG)
Tel: (41) 562981220

TAIWAN: Cactus Quality Co Ltd, 7FL-2, No 140, Roosevelt Road, Sec 2,Taipei, Taiwan, R.O.C.
Tel: 886-2-23656527 Email: cqcl@m17.hinet.net

THAILAND: Global Wide Trading, 10 Lad Prao Soi 88, Bangkok 10310. Tel: 00 662 933 9019
Email: global.wide@yahoo.com

U.S.A: Westminster Fibers Inc, 8 Shelter Drive, Greer South Carolina, NH03060.
Tel: 800 445-9276
Email: rowan@westminsterfibers.com

U.K: Rowan, Green Lane Mill, Holmfirth, West Yorkshire, England HD9 2DX.
Tel: +44 (0) 1484 681881 Fax: +44 (0) 1484 687920
Email: mail@knitrowan.com
Web: www.knitrowan.com

TEMPLATES

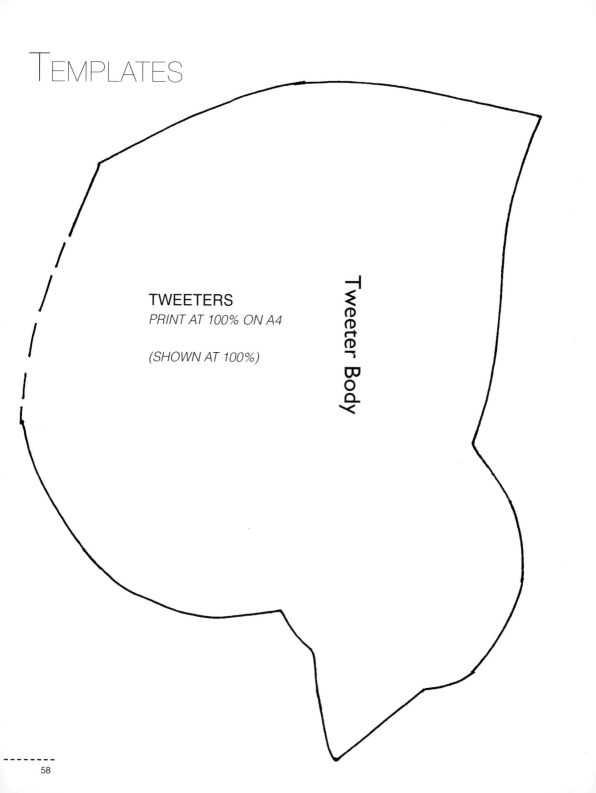

TWEETERS
PRINT AT 100% ON A4

(SHOWN AT 100%)

Tweeter Body

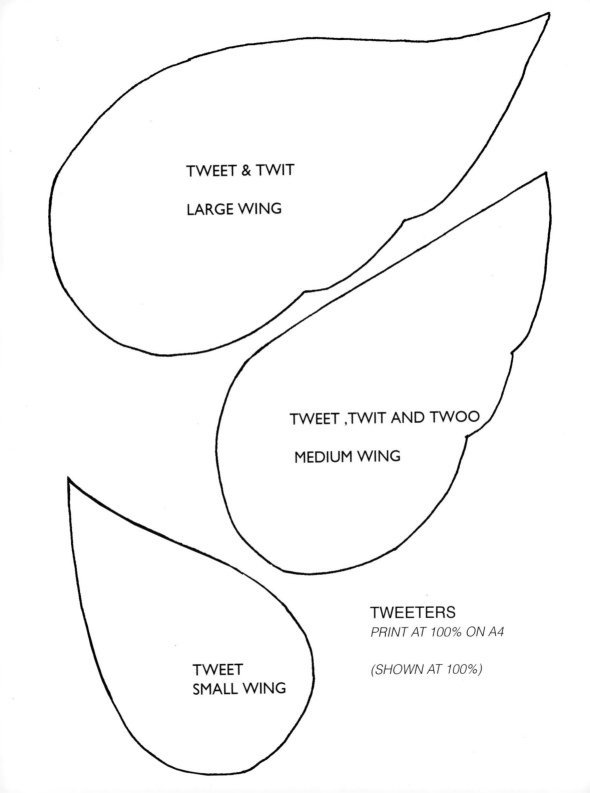

TWEET & TWIT

LARGE WING

TWEET ,TWIT AND TWOO

MEDIUM WING

TWEETERS
PRINT AT 100% ON A4

(SHOWN AT 100%)

TWEET
SMALL WING

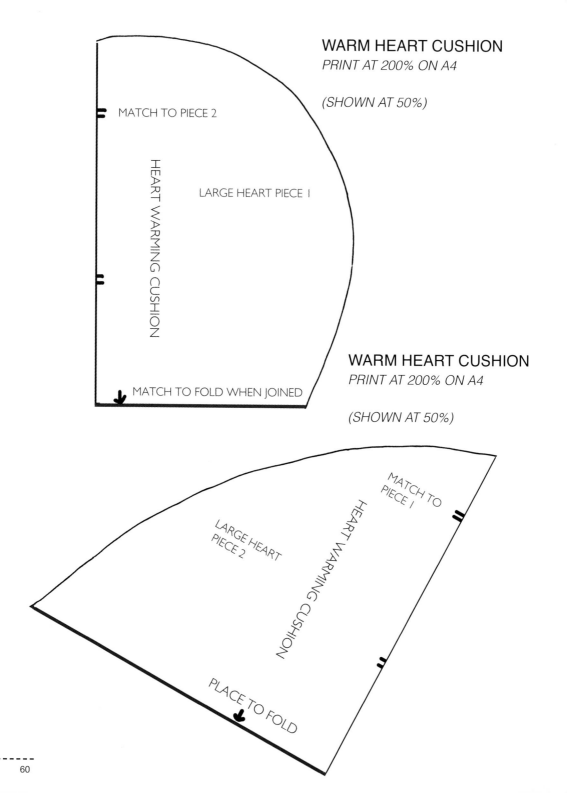

WARM HEART CUSHION
PRINT AT 200% ON A4

(SHOWN AT 50%)

MATCH TO PIECE 2

HEART WARMING CUSHION

LARGE HEART PIECE 1

MATCH TO FOLD WHEN JOINED

WARM HEART CUSHION
PRINT AT 200% ON A4

(SHOWN AT 50%)

MATCH TO PIECE 1

LARGE HEART PIECE 2

HEART WARMING CUSHION

PLACE TO FOLD

WARM HEART CUSHION
PRINT AT 200% ON A4

(SHOWN AT 50%)

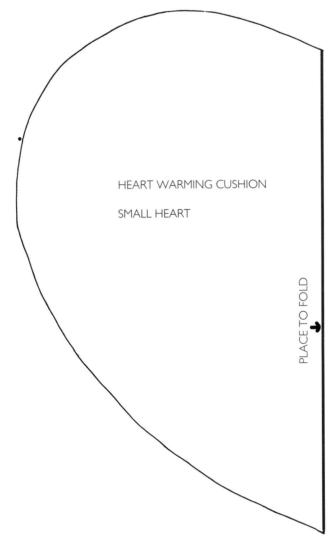

HEART WARMING CUSHION

SMALL HEART

PLACE TO FOLD

BUNTING
PRINT AT 100% ON A4

(SHOWN AT 100%)

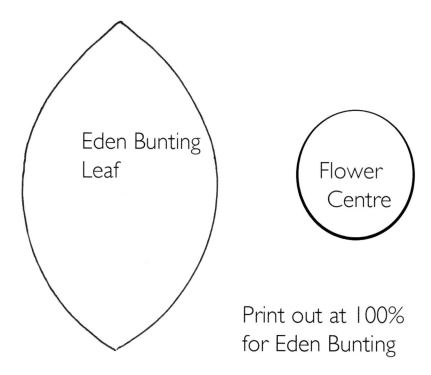

Eden Bunting
Leaf

Flower
Centre

Print out at 100%
for Eden Bunting

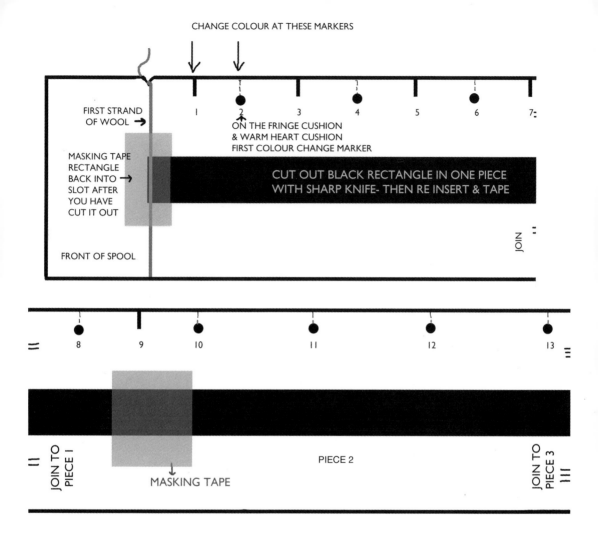

CHANGE COLOUR AT THESE MARKERS

FIRST STRAND OF WOOL →

1   2   3   4   5   6   7

ON THE FRINGE CUSHION
& WARM HEART CUSHION
FIRST COLOUR CHANGE MARKER

MASKING TAPE
RECTANGLE
BACK INTO →
SLOT AFTER
YOU HAVE
CUT IT OUT

CUT OUT BLACK RECTANGLE IN ONE PIECE
WITH SHARP KNIFE- THEN RE INSERT & TAPE

JOIN

FRONT OF SPOOL

8   9   10   11   12   13

JOIN TO PIECE 1

MASKING TAPE

PIECE 2

JOIN TO PIECE 3

ON THE FRINGE CUSHION

PRINT AT 200% ON A4

(SHOWN AT 50%)

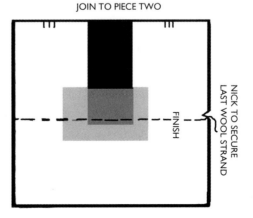

JOIN TO PIECE TWO

FINISH

NICK TO SECURE
LAST WOOL STRAND

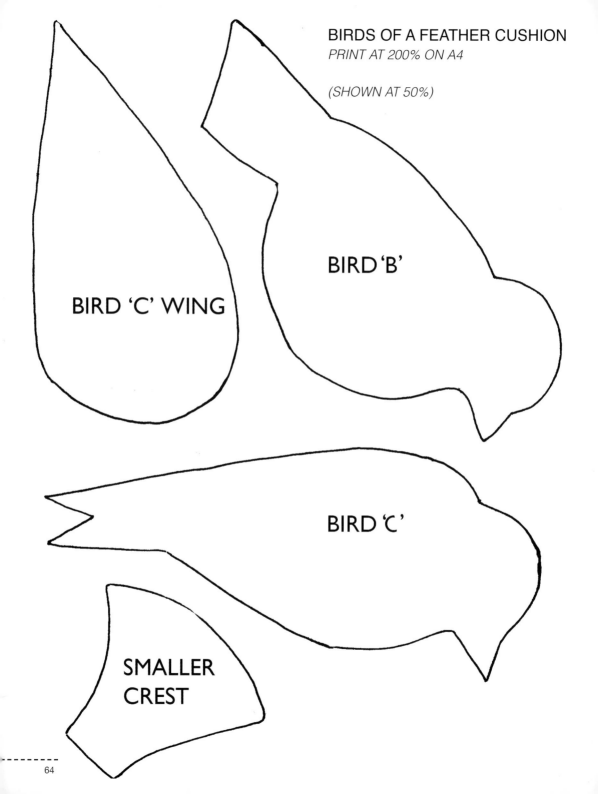

BIRDS OF A FEATHER CUSHION
PRINT AT 200% ON A4

(SHOWN AT 50%)

BIRD 'B'

BIRD 'C' WING

BIRD 'C'

SMALLER
CREST

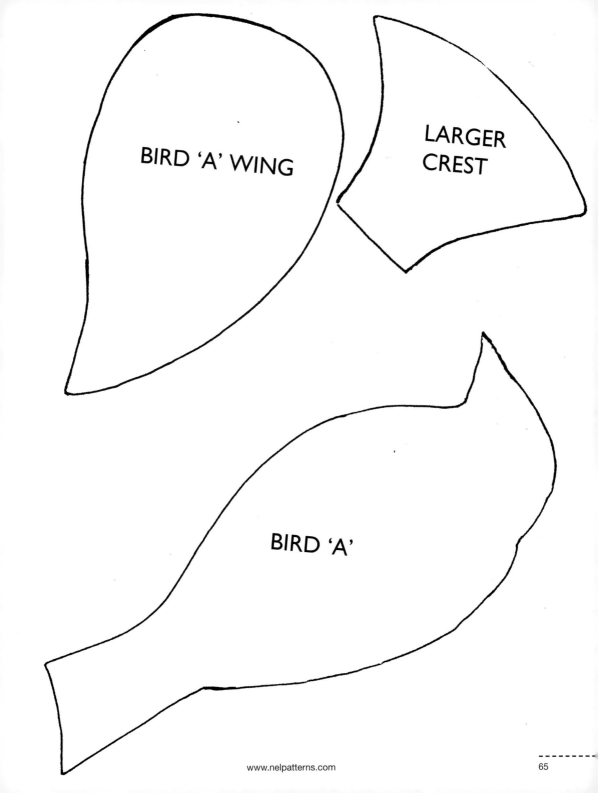

BIRD 'A' WING

LARGER CREST

BIRD 'A'

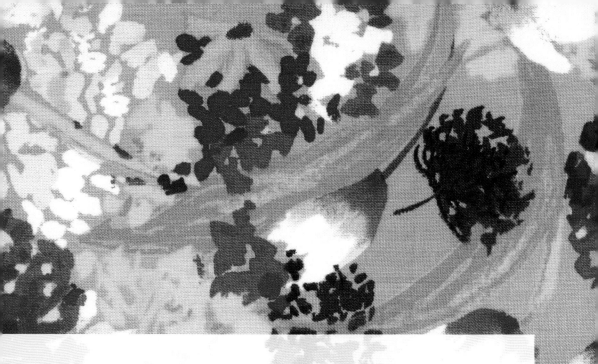

ACKNOWLEDGMENTS

This is the first Little Designer Guide so I do have to thank a few people, if you could bear with me! Firstly my family for the hours they didn't see me while I was writing this and making the projects. To Darren for being so easy to work with and for his continued enthusiasm for supporting English Designers. Joyce at Westminster Fibres for believing in me and my paintings. Everyone at Coats and Westminster for all the long hours they put in to promoting their designers. With much thanks also to Margaret Rowan, Katy Allaway and Christine Down for their expertise and sewing skills. Finally to my Mum and Dad for buying me my first easel and for encouraging me to go and study Art rather than Geography, as they believed that you should do what makes your heart sing and be brave. Lastly to Helen Wrightson, Polly Morris and Rebecca de Mendonca for being my creative hub your are priceless.